IN CHARGE

D1502604

IN CHARGE

A Complete Handbook for Kids with Working Parents

by KATHY S. KYTE

Drawings by Susan Detrich

Alfred A. Knopf, New York

THIS IS A BORZOI BOOK
PUBLISHED BY ALFRED A. KNOPF, INC.

Manufactured in the United States of America
Book design by Mina Greenstein

1   3   5   7   9   10   8   6   4   2

Library of Congress Cataloging in Publication Data
Kyte, Kathleen Sharar. In charge, a complete handbook
for kids with working parents.
Summary: Advice for children who must take care of themselves in the morning or after school on dealing with organizing
of time, fire, first aid, cooking (includes recipes), laundering and
mending clothes, and otherwise getting through the day. 1.
Latchkey children—Life skills guides. 2. Home economics.
[1. Latchkey children. 2. Children of working parents.
3. Life skills. 4. Home economics] I. Detrich, Susan, ill.
II. Title. HQ777.65.K97   1983   640'.024054 82-17927
ISBN 0-394-85408-X   ISBN 0-394-95408-4 (lib. bdg.)

To Michael, Brendan and Brooke,
with many thanks for their love and support,
and to Frances, with deepest appreciation.

Contents

Introduction

You're not alone. There are more than two million kids in America who get themselves off to school in the morning and take care of themselves (and sometimes younger brothers and sisters as well) after school or during school vacations because their parents are at work.

Every day, these kids are doing things they've never had to do before—things they may have thought they couldn't do on their own. They are finding out that they're *not* helpless. They *can* make their own beds, breakfasts, even decisions—and the result isn't disaster but, instead, a growing list of achievements and feelings of independence and pride.

You may have already experienced the satisfaction of doing some things for yourself. If you have, you are probably eager to learn more skills. You may be interested in first aid or emergency practices or in "taste testing" a new recipe.

Or you could be a newcomer to this group looking for ways to understand and organize your new responsibilities. You may need ideas for setting up a family conference or drawing up a daily schedule.

This book is for both groups—the "beginners" and the "old pros." It's for all kids who want to be informed, organized, and prepared for *any* event in their full, challenging, In Charge lives.

1. GETTING ORGANIZED

Family Conference

- Setting House Rules
- Discussing Expectations
- Choosing a Contact Person
- Preparing a Master Phone List
- Writing a Daily Schedule
- Dividing Chores
- Making Chore Schedules
- Assembling the In Charge "Tool Kit"

After the Conference— Organizing Yourself

- Organizing Your Time
- Organizing Your Space

Before you can take charge of any situation, you need to
know what the situation is. You need to find out what
is expected of you and what you can expect of others, what
rules and guidelines you will follow, what chores you will do
and when you will do them, and how and where you can get
help if you need it. This is the organizational foundation you
need for your In Charge life. You can lay some of this ground-
work on your own, but some must be done with your family.
The best way to work out family organization is at a family
conference. It will be easier and faster for you to get the information you need if everyone is together, *and* it will help family
understanding if members share in a discussion about household rules, responsibilities, and expectations.

Family Conference

Some families hold regular conferences, some hold them only
"as needed," and many families have never held a conference
or felt the need for one.

If your family already holds conferences, you can ask to have your organizational questions discussed at the next meeting (or meetings, if you have a lot of questions).

If your family has never held a conference, you may need to "sell" them on the idea. Explain how important it is to you, briefly describe the things you'd like to discuss, and suggest several possible days and times. The adult members of working families are often very short of free time. Offer to help them with a household chore or do a chore for them to gain an hour or two for a conference.

You can help the conference run more smoothly if you prepare a list of discussion topics in advance. Read through this section to get ideas, and then think about *your* concerns and add your own questions.

Setting House Rules

Every family has rules. You probably already know your family's rules by heart, but you need to find out if the rules change when you are In Charge. Prevent misunderstandings by asking questions. Here are some ideas:

- May you have friends over after school? Which friends? How often may they come over, and how long may they stay?
- Are there rules for use of the telephone? How often may you talk on it, and for how long?
- What about the television or stereo? Are there limits to how long you may watch or listen to them, and how loud they may be?
- Is there any appliance you should *not* use?

- Is it okay to go to a friend's house without calling a parent? What time should you return?
- If you are In Charge of younger children, you need to know what rules apply to them. May *they* have friends over, watch television, use the phone?

You can probably think of lots of other questions. How about snacks (what to eat, what not to eat) and homework (when to do it)?

Write down your family's House Rules so that you can refer to them later. And refer younger children to them if you need to.

Discussing Expectations

Another important item of business at your family conference should be a discussion about what family members expect of one another. You should know:

- *Exactly what's expected of you.* What are you In Charge of? Yourself, certainly, and maybe even younger brothers and sisters; but what about the housework, the meals, or the laundry? Are you supposed to assume a full share of responsibility for them too? Look at your schedule and those of other family members. What seems fair? What are you comfortable doing—or *not* comfortable doing? It's important to fully understand the role you will play in your working family.

- *If you are In Charge of younger children:* How much authority do you have? What decisions can you make, what orders can you give? This will probably depend on your age and the age of the younger children. It's important that everyone understand your role now so that there will be fewer disagreements later.

Choosing a Contact Person

You and your parents should select a neighbor to be your "contact person" in case of an emergency. Your contact person should be someone who is home most of the time—a retired neighbor is one possibility. Try to find another neighbor to be an "alternate" in case you need help and your contact person is not at home. After you've made your choices—and your contact person and alternate have agreed to serve—write

down their complete names, addresses, and phone numbers. You'll need to include this information in your master list of phone numbers (see next section).

Even if you live in the country and your closest neighbors are not very close, you should ask your nearest trusted neighbor to be your contact person. Try to find an alternate too.

Preparing a Master Phone List

Make a list of important telephone numbers and keep it near the phone. Include the following numbers on the list:

- *Police. Fire. Ambulance.* In some communities, this is one number (usually an easy-to-learn 3-digit number). Find out if there is a central emergency number in your city!
- *Contact person and alternate.* Be sure to write down their full names and addresses as well as phone numbers.
- *Parents' work numbers.* Get the name and address of each parent's workplace, the name of the division or department in which each works, and the *complete* phone number— including the extension number.

Find out now when you *should* phone a parent at work. Some kids "check in" every day after school, some phone if they have special news to share, and some phone only in an emergency. What system do your parents prefer?

• *School office numbers.* You should record the number of your school office as well as the school phone numbers of your brothers and sisters.

• *After-school and after-work activity numbers.* Does a parent take a night class or do you take French horn lessons? Write down the numbers of all after-school and after-work activity locations.

• *Your doctor.*

• *Your dentist.*

• *Your health insurance company.* This is not a phone number, but the name of the company can be important if you or a brother or sister need medical care. You should also write down your insurance account or the membership number.

• *The nearest Poison Control center.* This is especially important if you are caring for younger children.

• *Superintendent, manager, or maintenance person* (if you live in an apartment).

- *Your veterinarian* (if you have a pet). Some cities have a "house call" service for sick or injured animals. Does yours? If you live on a farm, you'll need to know the name and number of the veterinarian your family uses for large animals, too.

Can you think of other essential numbers? How about those of other adults—relatives or family friends?

Make a "mini-list" of the *most* important numbers on your list (parents' work phone, contact person's phone, etc.) and keep it in your wallet or notebook.

Writing a Daily Schedule

You need to know when your family will be at home, when they will be away from home, and *where* they'll be when they aren't at home. You need to know *your* Daily Schedule, and your family needs to know it too. Get complete information (what time do adults start and finish their workday, what time do you and your brothers and sisters leave for and arrive home from school, what after-school or after-work activities does your family have?), and put it all together into one easy-to-read schedule. Leave room on your schedule to pencil in appointments or special events.

Remember when preparing your schedule that work hours can vary from day to day and that adults can work at more than one job. Be sure you get full information.

If a parent works on Saturday or Sunday or if your family has lots of weekend activities, make a seven-day schedule.

If a parent travels on business, leave room to pencil in flight numbers, hotel names, or other special "on the road" information.

★ DAILY SCHEDULE ★

	MOM	DAD	DYLAN	MEGAN
MON	Work, 9-5	Work, 8-4	School, 8:15-3	School, 8:45-3:15 Soccer, 4-5 (Grant Field)
TUES	Work, 9-5 Swim, 6-7 (YWCA)	Work, 8-4	School, 8:15-3 Scouts, 4-6 (School)	School, 8:45-3:15
WEDS	Work, 9-5	Work, 8-3 Class, 4-5 (Community College)	Band, 7:30-8:15 (School) School, 8:15-3	School, 8:45-3:15
THURS	Work, 9-5	Work, 8-5	School, 8:15-3	School, 8:45-3:15 Soccer, 4-5 (Grant Field)
FRI	Work, 9-5	Work, 8-4	School, 8:15-3 Piano, 3:30-4 (Music Center)	School, 8:45-3:15

Post your schedule in a handy location—near the phone or on the family bulletin board—and remember to update it from time to time.

Dividing Chores

There are probably as many ways to divide chores as there are chores to divide. No one way is better than any other, and what works wonderfully for one family may not work at all for another. If your family doesn't already have a system, discuss the systems below and decide what will work for you.

- *List all chores that need to be done each day and each week.* Be sure that everyone agrees with the terms you use in making your list. What do you *mean* when you say "cleaning the kitchen"? To one person, cleaning the kitchen might mean emptying the dishwasher and wiping the counters; to another, it could mean scrubbing the floor, scouring the sink, cleaning the oven, and washing the windows.

- *Are there some chores that your family has already worked out?* If your family *always* alternates dinner preparations, then you don't need to include it on your chore list, although you should include it in your Chore Schedule. Does your family have special arrangements for weekend meals—do you go out for pizza on Saturday or to Aunt Jill's for chicken on Sunday, or does everyone prepare weekend meals together? Take these arrangements into account, too, when making your chore list.

- *Just whose dog is it?* Is it your sister's dog, or does it belong to the whole family? If it's your sister's, then she is proba-

bly already responsible for it, but if it's the family dog—or cat or gerbils—then the care should be divided just like any other chore. Anyone who has ever fed, walked, and cleaned up after a German shepherd will tell you what a chore pet care can be! If taking care of the family pet is *your* chore, you should know when (and what and where) to feed it and when (and where) to walk it—and how to clean up after it. What will you do if Spot makes a spot on the new carpet? Ask a parent which cleaning supplies you should use. You will also need to take extra safety precautions if you are In Charge of a pet—watch out for the iron, the oven, the curling iron, etc., and put away anything poisonous.

Don't be discouraged by the length of your list. Remember, everyone is going to help! Here are some ways of dividing your completed list:

- *Some parents assign chores.* They take some of the jobs for themselves—usually the bigger, more difficult jobs—and ask the kids to do the rest, basing their assignments on the kids' ages and abilities. This system works well for many families, especially if kids are able to swap jobs or negotiate for jobs they like and are good at.

- *In other families, members choose jobs.* If one person loves to cook and another loves to clean and they are both willing to "pitch in" and do the other chores, this method works fine and saves the bother of more complicated means of chore division.

- *Some families draw chores.* All household tasks are written on slips of paper and put into a bowl. Then family members draw from the bowl. This adds adventure to chore division and, over time, "hard" and "easy" jobs are usually spread fairly evenly among family members. If you want to be sure that they are evenly distributed, you can put groups of tasks on each slip, including *both* "hard" and "easy" tasks. For example, you could put all kitchen cleaning on one slip, which would include "easy" jobs like wiping counters and "hard" jobs like scrubbing the floor.

If your family decides to use this system and you want to "sweeten" the pot, put in a slip of paper (or three or four slips) with a "treat" instead of a task. Promise a dozen fresh-baked cookies, breakfast in bed, or best of all, a day off from chores (other family members can do the winner's chores for a day).

Using Chore Scores

Some families use "chore scores" to divide tasks so that there is absolutely no doubt about the fairness of work distribution. Here's how the chore score system works:

Give each household task a point value from one to ten. Rate each job on its degree of boredom, difficulty, or overall "yuckiness." For instance, using this system, an easy job like dusting the piano would probably get a "one" rating, while scrubbing the basement floor might earn a "nine." The whole family must agree on the "point value" of each task. Once they've agreed and you've written the values beside each task on your chore list, total the points. *Now* divide the total by the number of people in your family. If you have 400 points and 2 family members, you will each have to choose 200 points worth of work.

✳ CHORE SCORE SHEET ✳

WEEKLY		DAILY		
Dust	3	Cook Breakfast	3	(x7)=21
Vacuum	5	Make Lunches	3	(x7)=21
Scrub Kitchen Floor	6	Cook Dinner	6	(x7)=42
Scrub Bathroom Floor	6	Breakfast Dishes	2	(x7)=14
Clean Shower, Sink, Toilet	8	Dinner Dishes	4	(x7)=28
Water Plants	2	Empty Garbage	3	(x7)=21
Laundry	8	Sweep Kitchen	2	(x7)=14
Ironing	6	Feed Cat, Clean Litter	3	(x7)=21
Grocery Shop	6	Straighten Living Room	2	(x7)=14
Total Weekly Tasks	50	Total Daily Tasks		196

GRAND TOTAL = 246

✳ Divided by 2 (Dad, Peter) = 123 Each ✳

Using this example, Dad and Peter each would pick which tasks they wanted to do for their 123 weekly points. Sometimes it might come out uneven—Peter might wind up with 110 points and Dad with 136—but they could make it up the next week or could do one or two tasks together to make the scores come out even.

Your family probably has more chores or fewer chores or different chores or different ideas about the point value of each chore, but you can still use the chore system if you like it. Just be sure that everyone agrees on the point values you assign to the tasks.

Of course, if there are very young children in your family, they aren't going to be able to do a full share of the work, and everyone should discuss what share they *can* handle. Even *very* little kids can help in some way (clearing clutter, setting the table, etc.), and they should be encouraged to help in any way they can.

You can use an abbreviated version of chore scores too. Divide all household jobs into "big," "medium," and "small." Each family member then picks a set amount of each kind of job (see example in the Chore Schedule below). Again, this system works well as long as everyone agrees upon what is "big," "medium," and "small." Cooking dinner may be only a "medium" job to you but a "huge" job to your sister.

No matter what system or chore assignment your family decides to use, it's important to remain flexible. You should be willing to shift jobs and discuss job assignments until everyone is satisfied with the distribution of household work. Remember, too, there are going to be times when your schedule changes, or another family member is ill, gone, or busy, and the schedule will have to be adjusted.

Making Chore Schedules

Once you've decided who is going to do what, you need to decide when they are going to do it. Discuss this at your family conference and then make a Chore Schedule and post it beside your family's Daily Schedule.

Your family may want a simple schedule, like this:

★ CHORE•SCHEDULE ★		
	EVERY DAY	ONCE A WEEK
JESSE	Breakfast Dishes Make Lunches Feed, Walk Dog	Vacuum House Laundry
MOM	Cook Dinner Sweep Kitchen Take out Trash	Ironing Clean Bathroom
MARY BETH	Cook Breakfast Dinner Dishes Straighten Den	Clean Kitchen Grocery Shop

A schedule that spells out each day's work might be better for your family.

CHORE SCHEDULE				
DAY OF THE WEEK	TEDDY	JULIE	MOM	DAD
MONDAY	Laundry Trash	Breakfast Dinner Dishes	Lunches Br. Dishes	Dinner
TUESDAY	Dinner	Lunches Br. Dishes	Breakfast Dinner Dishes	Vacuum Trash
WEDNESDAY	Lunches Dinner Dishes Trash	Dinner	Breakfast Br. Dishes	Ironing
THURSDAY	Dust Br. Dishes	Breakfast Dinner Dishes Clean Bathroom	Lunches Trash	Dinner Clean Kitchen
FRIDAY	Breakfast Dinner Dishes	Lunches Trash	Dinner	Grocery Shop Br. Dishes

Families who use the abbreviated form of chore scores (the "big," "medium," and "small" system) sometimes use a weekly sign-up sheet for their scheduling (see page 18).

Your family may want to stick to the same schedule for a week, a month, or a year. If you have a schedule that works well, and everyone is happy with the chore assignments, there's no reason to change.

In addition to deciding which days to do chores, many families want to decide what time of day chores will be done. This makes sense for a lot of chores. If Timmy is in charge of cleaning the bathroom, he should probably do it before (or after) ev-

CHORE SIGN-UP

★ SIGN UP BY FRIDAY

☆ PICK: 2 Weekly or 1 Daily BIG Jobs
2 Weekly or 1 Daily MEDIUM Jobs
3 Weekly or 2 Daily SMALL Jobs

Weekly BIG Jobs

Vacuum _____
Clean Bathroom _____
Clean Kitchen_____
Laundry _____
Ironing _____
Grocery Shop_____

Daily BIG Jobs

Cook Dinner_____

Weekly MEDIUM Jobs

Sweep Garage_____
Clean Car_____

Daily MEDIUM Jobs

Cook Breakfast_____
Make Lunches _____
Dinner Dishes_____
Walk Dog_____

Weekly SMALL Jobs

Water Plants _____
Dust _____
Bundle Newspapers _____

Daily SMALL Jobs

Breakfast Dishes_____
Sweep Kitchen _____
Straighten Living Room____
Feed Dog _____
Take out Trash _____
Feed Cat, Clean Litter____

eryone begins lining up for their evening (or morning) shower, and if Teri is in charge of sweeping the kitchen, she shouldn't do it while Dad's cooking dinner. There are good times to do chores and there are better times. Agree on the *best* time to do your chores.

If your chores include using any appliances—washer, dryer, stove, vacuum cleaner, or whatever—arrange for lessons. Find out how to operate the appliance, how to maintain it (change vacuum cleaner bags, empty washer and dryer lint traps, etc.), and what to do if the appliance *doesn't* operate. Does your clothes washer creak and whine when it is overloaded, or does a buzzer go off, or does it just tear up all of the clothes and dump

suds all over the floor? Find out now what habits, good and bad, your appliances have. Take notes during your lessons so that you can consult them later.

Assembling the In Charge "Tool Kit"

Understanding your family's rules and expectations helps prepare you for being In Charge. Beyond this, there are only a few things that you need to be a fully equipped In Charge kid. Here are some suggestions for your In Charge "tool kit." Talk them over with your family and see if they have further ideas.

• *The key.* Of course. Without the key you're a goner. Talk about the care and keeping of your key. Should you wear it on a chain or a string around your neck, carry it on a keychain, or slip it into a secret compartment in your billfold? Whatever you decide, *don't* wear it or carry it where everyone can see it (tuck it into your shirt if you wear it around your neck, carry it in your hand if it's on a keychain), and *don't* label it with your name, address, or phone number. It's tempting to label a key so that it will be returned if it is lost, but police say that this isn't safe.

Leave a spare key with your contact person or, if you live in an apartment, with your building's superintendent or manager. *Don't* hide a spare key outside your house or apartment.

• *Personal emergency fund.* Personal emergencies come in all shapes and sizes, but luckily they don't come along that often. A personal emergency is when you forget your lunch *and* your lunch money or when you miss your school bus or lose your bus pass or lock yourself out. If you're prepared, these won't *be* disasters, just inconveniences. Decide how much money you want to carry for "emergency insurance."

• *Household emergency fund.* This isn't for smoke and flame, bruised and bloody emergencies (those are covered in Chapter 2) but for routine, everyday household emergencies—for the times when you need a light bulb or a loaf of bread and the grocery fund is empty. A household emergency is when the newspaper carrier comes to collect for the third time and you've forgotten (again) to remind your parent to leave the money. A household emergency is when your little brother needs to buy the sheet music today for his piano recital tomorrow. Keep five to ten dollars tucked away in a cupboard.

- *Grocery fund* (or charge account). If you are going to buy groceries, you need to have money to do it or (better yet) have a charge account at a nearby grocery store. Some stores let regular customers "charge" groceries and then bill them monthly for their purchases. If a neighborhood store will do this for your family, it will eliminate the need for a grocery fund. Be sure that the grocer knows that you are authorized to charge on your family's account. If there is no store near you that offers this service, you should have a small amount of money to make grocery purchases. Try to avoid keeping too much money in the house, and don't tell anyone outside the family that you keep *any* cash around.
- *Supplies for family organization.* There are a few easily purchased items that will make your In Charge life easier and will help your family stay organized.

Both a chalkboard and a corkboard are handy for working families. You can post schedules and emergency numbers on the corkboard and jot down appointments, messages, or shopping reminders on the chalkboard. Family members can use the chalkboard to "keep in touch," letting one another know about a change of plans or schedules.

"In" and "Out" baskets—or boxes or trays—help keep your mail and messages straight. Store a pair near the front door and put incoming mail, messages from school, etc., into the "In" basket. Outgoing mail, signed permission slips, and the like go in the "Out" basket. If everyone makes a point of checking these as they enter and leave, information is less likely to be forgotten or lost.

Can you think of other organizational supplies? How about a hook for the dog's leash near the front door, an envelope in the kitchen for dry cleaning receipts and another for coupons or trading stamps?

What else does your family want to include in *your* "tool kit"? Don't forget this book!

Concluding the Conference

Before the conference ends, make sure that you have all the information you need. If you have doubts about schedules, rules, or expectations, discuss them now while everyone is together. You may find that you have so many questions and ideas that one conference is not enough. Do you need to schedule another conference or two to finish up?

If this was your first family conference, it might be helpful if you talk about the experience. How did the discussion go? Did everyone participate, or did one or two people do most of the talking? A conference "leader" can help keep the discussion moving smoothly and can keep everyone on the subject and make sure that everyone gets an opportunity to speak. You can draw straws to choose a leader for each conference.

Were there disagreements or arguments at your conference? That's perfectly normal; you shouldn't expect complete agreement. If everyone agreed completely about everything, there wouldn't be much point in having a conference. Disagreements are fine as long as you are eventually able to reach a solution that everyone is comfortable with. This is more likely if you or the conference leader make sure that everyone gets a fair hearing (equal time). It helps, too, if everyone remembers that the purpose of a family conference is not to win an argument but to work together to solve family problems.

If your family wants to hold regular family conferences, you can help organize them if you keep a list of discussion topics. Pin a piece of paper to the bulletin board and remind everyone to jot down topics as they think of them.

Family conferences take time—and a little effort—but they are a good way for working families to find ways of reaching shared goals.

After the Conference— Organizing Yourself

There is a lot that you can do on your own to get organized. Some of it's simple stuff, like remembering to put your belongings away in the proper place. And some of it's more complicated, like learning to make (and stick to) a personal schedule. Here are some ideas to help you get started.

Organizing Your Time

Now that you have your schedule or chore list with *all those* chores, and you have *all those* free hours after school and on weekends, you need to figure out how to fit the two together into a hassle-free personal schedule. Being In Charge means that you use your time wisely—you do your homework in the afternoon or early evening (before you become too tired to do it well), and you do your household chores promptly so that they don't hang over your day like a dark cloud.

- *Make a personal schedule.* It isn't easy to learn to manage time, and it will take you a while to get the hang of it. Don't get discouraged—many adults are still wrestling with the problem! It helps, when you are still learning time management, to make a list of everything you have to do each day. Next, estimate how long it will take. Be generous in your time estimate, especially if you haven't done the work before. Next, look at your available time (time when you aren't in school or busy with music lessons, sports, etc.). Now decide when the best time is for each job on your list. When's the best time to scrub the kitchen floor

(is there a time when you are scheduled to scrub it)? Do you always need help with math homework? If so, schedule it for a time when someone will be available to help you. After you've decided on the time that you feel is best for each item on your "must do" list, make up a personal schedule.

If your schedule changes from day to day (if you have piano lessons at 3 P.M. on Tuesdays and judo lessons at 4 P.M. on Fridays, for example), you will want to make up a new schedule each evening for the following day (it only takes a minute once you have the hang of it). If your schedule remains pretty much the same from day to day, you

● ANDREA'S SCHEDULE ●

6:15 AM	Get up, Make Bed, Shower, Dress
	Cook and Eat Breakfast
8:00	Leave for School
3:30 PM	Arrive Home from School
4-5	Track Practice
5:15	Arrive Home from Track Practice
5:30-6:30	Homework
6:30-7:30	Eat Dinner, Wash Dinner Dishes
7:30-9:00	Homework
9 - 10:30	Read, Watch Television
10:30	Bed

★ NICKY'S SCHEDULE ★

6:45 AM	Get up, Make Bed, Dress
	Eat Breakfast
	Wash Breakfast Dishes
	Take out Trash
8:15	Leave for School
3:45 PM	Arrive Home from School
4:30-5:30	Homework
5:30-6:30	Cook, Eat Dinner
7-8	Choir Practice
8:30-9	Homework
9-9:30	Shower
9:30-10	Read, Watch Television
10:00	Bed

can make up one schedule for the whole week. Try to stick to your personal schedule while you're learning to budget time. Later you probably won't need a schedule.

- *Make a list*—of things you absolutely can't forget. You may find at first that you need a "school" list and a "home" list if you have things you must remember in both locations. Just as with the schedule, you may not need these "memory joggers" after a while, but they are helpful when you are first taking charge.

- *Set reasonable goals for yourself.* You will only be frustrated and unhappy if you expect to mow the lawn, do your homework, play basketball, and take out the trash in two hours. Think about what you *can* do, not what you *wish* you could do.

- *Speak up.* If you find that you aren't able to keep up with school, other activities, and your household chores, it's important to let your family know. For instance, if you are snowed under with algebra this semester, you should ask your family to redistribute chores until you get on top of your schoolwork. Remember, you're the only one who can judge how much time you need, and you're the only one who can ask for more time.

- *Give yourself time to relax.* Most In Charge kids are terrific about doing their homework and their housework, but some seem to have a hard time taking it easy. You don't have to work every minute to prove you're responsible. Make time on each day's list for "being a kid."

Organizing Your Space

This is a good time to look over your room and find ways to "streamline" it for easier care. If you share a room with a sister or brother, make this a joint project.

- *Start with a good cleaning.*

   Take the room apart. Dump drawers, empty closets, pull things out from under the bed. Get all your belongings out where you can see them.

   Next, sort out everything you've outgrown—clothes that are too small, toys and games that you are too old for. Put the things that are in good shape in one stack and things that are broken or torn beyond repair in a trash bag. Good outgrown items can be "passed down" or, if you have no younger brothers or sisters and lots of outgrown items, think about having a garage, porch, or yard sale.

Go through and weed out dirty clothes. Put them in the laundry hamper or on a pile for dry cleaning.

Put things that need repair—clothes that need mending, shoes that need laces, books that need taping—into a "fix-it" box. Take time to mend them soon!

Now group belongings by type—socks in one stack, books in another, etc.—until everything is sorted and grouped.

All you have to do now is put everything away, *but* be sure that you put things away according to type and put them in logical locations. What do you need *every* day?

Put these items in the top drawers, the front of the closet, and reserve the lower drawers and hard-to-reach closet shelves for things you don't need often. If it's winter, store your snowshoes in the front of the closet and your ski sweaters in the top drawers, and put your water skis and bathing suits in the back of the closet. "Rotate" your storage with the changing of the seasons.

• *Now here are some suggestions to keep you organized.*

Keep your school supplies in a desk drawer or in a box or basket near the place where you usually do your homework.

Store your sports equipment in a basket near the door or hang it on a pegboard on the wall, using net bags to hold balls and other "hard to hang" items.

Put a row of pegs or an expandable "mug rack" on the back of the door or on a wall near the door. Use it for your coat, umbrella, bag or backpack.

A corkboard in your room is handy for your own schedule, lists, and notes to yourself.

A set of "In" and "Out" baskets or trays for your desk or work area will help you keep track of homework, letters, etc.

Make sure that you have a good supply of hangers in your closet—special pants and skirt hangers make it easy to hang these items up.

A laundry hamper for your room might make it easier to get the socks off the floor and into the wash. Make it *your* job to empty it into the family hamper or carry it to the laundry room.

- *Take a minute.* Hang clothing up, put things away neatly. It may take an extra minute now, but it can save you *hours* later!

- *Keep a list.* Jot down school supplies, clothing, or other things you need. Do *all* your socks have holes in them? Write it down and see about getting new ones. Maybe your family should start a "Master Shopping List" for everyone to write down their personal needs as well as household items.

- *Spread the good word.* Now that you've organized your own space, head up a weekend work party to tackle the

whole house or apartment. Use the same cleaning and organizing tactics you used on your room.

Don't stop now. Keep looking for ways to organize, reorganize, and improve your own and your family's chores, schedules, and space. Write down your ideas (*another* list) and call for another family conference.

2. COPING WITH A CRISIS

Minor Crisis

- Lockout
- Blackout
- Plumbing

Major Crisis

- Fire
- Crime
- First Aid and Medical

Emergencies don't occur very often, and chances are good that you will never need most of the information in this chapter—but read through it anyway. The skills you'll learn will help you get through any crisis with confidence, and the chapter's prevention tips may help you avoid a crisis to begin with.

The first rule of crisis management is to "stay calm." This rule applies to "mini" crises, like forgetting your lunch or your key, and to "maxi" crises, like fires, accidents, or prowlers. Educate yourself about emergency procedures, plan *exactly* what you would do in an emergency, and stay calm if one arises. You will astonish yourself with your In Charge, crisis-coping ability.

Minor Crisis

Minor crises are irritating, but they aren't the end of the world. No one's bleeding, nothing's smoking or flaming. Put these crises in perspective, and think of them as opportunities to polish your crisis-management skills.

Lockout

It only *seems* like the end of the world. Nearly everyone has been locked out at one time or another, though. Plan ahead— leave a spare key with your contact person. If you live in an apartment, you can also leave a spare with your building's superintendent or manager. Then, if you are locked out, all you have to do is retrieve your spare key and let yourself in. Remember to return the key so that it's available for the next lockout!

If you are locked out and haven't left a spare key with anyone, go to a neighbor's and phone a parent. If there are no neighbors at home, use your "disaster money" to phone a parent from a pay phone.

Blackout

• *Prepare for a blackout.* Keep a flashlight or two in a handy location. Test the batteries occasionally, but use the flash-

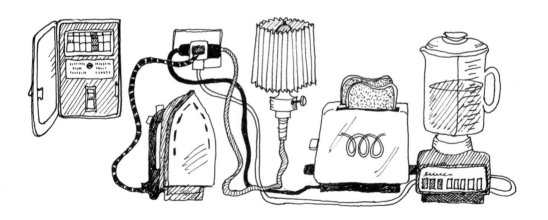

light(s) for emergencies only. Don't plan to use candles in a blackout. They don't throw off enough light to be very useful, and they are a fire hazard.

- *Find out where your home's circuit-breaker box or fuse box is.* Electric current for your house or apartment is controlled through one of these boxes, and it is sometimes, although not often, necessary to reset the box if a circuit breaker is tripped or a fuse is blown by overloading it (using too many electrical appliances at once). Resetting is not complicated, and you can learn to do it.

  While you are getting acquainted with your circuit breaker or fuse box, label each breaker or fuse so that you can quickly identify which appliance or part of your home it controls. This is useful in evaluating a blackout and can be essential in case of electric shock (see First Aid section, page 58).

- *If the power does go off when you are In Charge.* Determine if the power outage affects the whole neighborhood or just your home. Look out the window, or if that doesn't help, phone your contact person and other neighbors and ask if their houses have power.

- *If the whole neighborhood is without power.* If there is no obvious reason for the blackout—like a snow, wind, or rainstorm—sit tight for a few minutes and the power will probably come back on. If it isn't back on soon, or if you're really worried, this might be a good time to pay a friendly visit to your contact neighbor.

- *If your house or apartment is the only one without power.* Determine if the whole house or apartment is affected or only a part of it. If it affects the whole house or apartment, phone a parent or consult your contact neighbor. If you

live in an apartment, phone your building's superintendent, maintenance worker, or manager. If only one area or
appliance is affected, and if you've had lessons in resetting
the breaker or fuse box, fix it yourself. Before resetting,
turn off all appliances and lights—and take care not to
overload once the breaker or fuse is fixed.

Plumbing

- *Know where the main water shutoff is in your home.* Just
  as the circuit breaker or fuse box is often the "magic key"
  to electrical problems, the water shutoff is often the key to
  plumbing problems. It is located at the point where the
  main water pipe enters your home from the street. A parent can help you find it. Once you've located it, practice
  turning it on and off, and mark it with a bright piece of
  yarn or colored tape so that you can find it quickly in an
  emergency.

MAIN
SHUT-
OFF
VALVE

- *Most modern homes also have individual shutoff valves for each sink and toilet.* Find and mark them. Older homes don't always have shutoff valves, and if yours doesn't, you'll just have to be prepared to run for the main shutoff if there's a plumbing emergency.
- *If a pipe begins to leak badly or bursts, or if the toilet begins to overflow.* Use individual or main shutoffs, then phone a parent. They might want to phone a plumber.
- *Call the superintendent, manager, or maintenance person.* If you live in an apartment and have plumbing problems, these are the people to call—but act first. Shut off water, *then* phone.

Major Crisis

A major crisis requires immediate clear-headed action. The most important thing you can do *now* to guarantee you will be ready for any major crisis is to think about emergency situations and talk about them with your family. Talking about emergencies may be awkward at first—your parents would like to protect you from *anything* unpleasant—but, in the long run, it will make you a lot more comfortable and confident of your ability to be In Charge.

Fire

No one wants to talk about fire. Most people find fire so frightening, they don't even want to *think* about it. That's not only silly, it's dangerous. Fire officials say that proper planning could save *thousands* of lives every year.

There are many things that you can do to reduce your chances of becoming a victim of a home fire.

• *Know your escape routes.* Walk from room to room in your house or apartment, noting *exactly* where the doors and windows are. Close your eyes. Could you find the doors and windows in the dark or if the room was filled with smoke? Open the windows in each room. Which ones actually open, and which ones are painted or nailed shut or are blocked from the outside by screens, storm windows, or security grates? Once you have the window open, look

down. How far from the ground are the windows? You should *not* attempt to jump from a window above the second floor unless instructed to do so at the time of a fire, but you *can* use upper-story windows to alert neighbors and call for help.

- *Which exit is the best for each room, and which is the second-best?* If you live in an apartment, where are your building's fire escapes and where is the nearest stairway? You should *not* use an elevator if there is a fire.

  If you are In Charge of younger children, have them explore each room with you. They should understand that learning the exits is very important and could save their lives, but you don't have to make the activity frightening for them. Make sure that they know which windows open and how to open them. Some families make "escape maps" to check their accuracy at designing safe routes out of a home fire.

- *Hold a fire drill.* Yes, just like at school. Explain to your family that you need to test your escape skills.

- *Give your home a fire inspection.* Watch for the following fire hazards: clothing, rags, or other burnable items stored near heating equipment; newspapers or oily rags stored in an unventilated area (like an attic or closet); an unscreened fireplace; frayed cords on electric appliances; or matches left within the reach of small children. Move or throw away flammable items (such as painting and cleaning supplies) stored near a furnace and combustible items (such as oily rags and newspapers) stored in closed spaces; buy a fireplace screen (or don't use the fireplace); have appliance cords repaired; and keep matches and lighters away from children. Take a good look around—can you find other hazards? Many fire departments will provide you with a free list of things to look for, and some will even send inspectors out to give your house or apartment a "top-to-bottom" safety check.

• *Equip your home with fire safety "tools."* Smoke alarms save lives. Smoke is the real danger in a fire. Smoke is made up of poisonous gases, and many more people are killed by smoke inhalation than are killed by fire. However, there are now reasonably priced smoke alarms available to warn residents when smoke is building to dangerous levels. A smoke alarm is often the first signal you have of a home fire and should alert you to get out fast. Smoke alarms are required by law in some states.

A home fire extinguisher can be used to put out a small home fire *before* it becomes a major fire. Extinguishers are essential for electrical or grease fires where water can't be used. Fire officials recommend that homes have at least one extinguisher—preferably hung on a kitchen wall.

Many department and hardware stores sell ladders which hook to window walls and can help you escape from a second-story window. If you do buy one of these ladders, find out how to hook it safely to the window sill and store it near the window you would use in an emergency.

• *Be careful.* You can help prevent fires by using good sense. Practice kitchen safety, take care if you must use matches, don't use appliances with frayed or worn cords or plugs, and keep an eye on younger children in your care.

Putting Out Small Fires

- *Only you can judge whether or not you can safely put out a fire.* If it is quite small and reasonably contained (in a wastebasket, for example), try to put it out with water or with your home fire extinguisher. If the fire is not small or is growing, remember how quickly fire spreads and get out fast!
- *Never* use water on a grease or electrical fire.

Putting Out Clothing Fires

- *If you are with someone whose clothing catches fire.* Push them to the ground or floor and roll them in a rug, blanket, or coat to smother the flames. Burn treatment is discussed on page 54.
- *If your own clothing catches fire.* Drop to the floor or ground and roll to smother the flames.

Escaping a Home Fire

- *If you see fire, if you smell smoke, or if your smoke alarm begins to sound.* If the fire is not small enough for you to put out, leave immediately. Go to a neighbor's home and phone the fire department. If you are In Charge of younger children, lead them out. If you are separated from them by the fire, call to them to leave by their own escape routes and get out yourself and go for help.
- *If there are closed doors between you and the exit.* Feel each door before opening it. If it is cool, open it slowly. If it is hot, find another escape route.

- *If you have to leave through a smoke-filled room.* Remember that smoke rises, and crawl quickly to the nearest exit.
- *If you have to jump.* Don't jump from windows higher than the second floor unless told to do so by fire officials. If you are trapped above the second floor, stuff blankets, towels, or clothing under the door, open a window, and call for help. Remain near the window until help arrives.
- *Once you are out of a burning building.* Never go back in. No possession—not even a loved pet—is worth your life.

Crime

No one needs to tell you that crime rates are rising. Newspaper headlines and television reports make it sound as though we're in the middle of a crime epidemic. This shouldn't frighten you, but it should make you careful and encourage you to learn about crime prevention. Common sense and reasonable caution can protect you from most crime.

There are crime prevention measures that you can carry out with your family, as well as some steps you can take on your own.

Family Crime Prevention

- *Mark your belongings.* Police say that it discourages burglars if property owners engrave their possessions—using a driver's license or social security number for identification—and put stickers on their windows and doors letting would-be burglars know that property is engraved and can be traced. Some police departments will loan engravers. Inexpensive engravers are also sold in many hardware stores. The stickers are available through the police or with engravers.

- *Don't hide spare keys outside.* The cleverest hiding places are ones that have been used over and over again, and a would-be burglar can find them without difficulty.

- *Don't store ladders outside.* Put away ladders, stools, or anything else that could be used to help a would-be burglar climb through a window. Trim away tree limbs close to windows.

- *Don't invite trouble.* Don't keep large amounts of cash or valuable jewelry around the house.

- *Keep hedges and shrubs trimmed.* Don't offer burglars a hiding place. Keep shrubs back from windows and doors, too, so that neighbors can keep an eye on your home.

- *Get to know your neighbors.* Agree to watch one another's homes, and report anything suspicious to the police. The "nosy neighbor" policy pays off in reduced crime rates!

- *Check your locks.* If you aren't sure whether your locks are safe, ask your police department. Some police departments will send officers to do a security check on your whole home!

Personal Crime Prevention

- *Lock before leaving.* Before you leave home, make sure that *all* windows and doors are closed and locked.

- *Do a homecoming check.* If your house or apartment looks different when you come home than it looked when you left it—if a door or window is open, for example—don't go inside. Go to a neighbor's and phone home (to see if a family member has come home unexpectedly). If there's no answer, phone a parent (to see if someone *has* been at home). If a parent recommends it, you should phone the police.

- *Lock up.* Once you are inside your home, lock the door and keep it locked.

- *Don't open the door for strangers.* If your door doesn't have a peephole viewer, ask *through the door* who it is. *Don't* open the door with the chain on—most chains are actually very little protection against someone forcing the door.

  Tell strangers who come to your door that your mother or father is busy and can't come to the door right now. Say that they're in the shower or on the phone or taking a nap. If the person doesn't leave right away or argues with you, go to the phone and call your contact neighbor or the police.

Don't be fooled by requests to use your bathroom or telephone. Say that your mother or father is using it.

If someone says he is making a delivery or is supposed to repair something in your home—and you weren't told to expect a delivery or repair-person—don't let him in. It doesn't matter if the person is wearing a uniform, carrying a tool box, flashing an identification card, carrying a bouquet of roses, or leading a herd of camels. If you weren't expecting anyone, *don't* let anyone in. Tell the person *firmly* but politely that you are sorry but you weren't told to expect a delivery or repair-person and that your mother, father, or 300-pound uncle is in bed, in the bathtub, or in the basement breaking bricks with their bare hands and you were told not to disturb them, *no matter what.* Tell the person that you will have your parent call him later. *Do* call a parent when the person has gone so that legitimate repairs and deliveries can be rescheduled. As with any stranger, if the person argues with you or doesn't leave right away, go to the phone and call your contact neighbor and/or the police.

It's probably safer to arrange deliveries and repairs for times when an adult will be at home, but that isn't always possible. If you are expecting a delivery or repair-person, have him slip an identification card under the door or into the mail chute; then call the shop or store to confirm the identification *before* you open the door.

You can try to minimize the possibility of having to deal with strangers at your door by putting a sign on the door saying that you don't want to be disturbed by salespeople. You're not likely to buy anything without your parents' permission, anyway, and salespeople will only be a hassle to deal with.

Above all, don't be embarrassed by your refusal to answer the door or let people in. We are all raised to have good manners and to be helpful and friendly, but that *doesn't* mean that you have to take silly chances. Remember, it's *your* house, *you're* In Charge.

• *Take charge of the phone.* If a stranger calls while you're home alone, say that your mother or father is busy and will return the call later. Take the person's name and phone number and hang up. Never give *your* name, phone number, address, or *any other* information about yourself or your family to anyone on the phone. If a caller should ask, say that you're not allowed to give that information, then hang up.

Never give a "wrong" number your right number. If the caller asks, "What number is this?" you say, "What number were you calling?"

If you pick up the phone and no one speaks right away or if someone begins to speak in an obscene manner, hang up immediately. If you don't act frightened or shocked, it will deprive such callers of the thrill they are after, and they will be less likely to call again. If this kind of call continues, phone a parent, your contact neighbor, or the telephone company.

If There Is a Prowler

• *If you are in the house and someone is trying to get in.* Leave by another exit and go to a neighbor's and phone the police. Burglars and prowlers aren't usually anxious for a confrontation, so make a calm, quiet, and quick exit.

- *If you can't get out safely.* Phone the police and lock yourself in a room. Sit very quietly and wait for the police to arrive.
- *When you phone the police.* Tell them that there is a "burglary *in progress*" and give them your *full* name, address, and telephone number.

First Aid and Medical Procedures

In any injury or medical crisis, you must stay cool, do what you can, and know when to get help. If you read this section carefully, you will be equipped to handle the most common first aid and medical emergencies.

First Aid Kit

A good first aid kit will help you through any minor medical emergency. There's something reassuring about just knowing that you *have* one. Buy a first aid kit or assemble one yourself. If you decide to "do-it-yourself," include:

a box of Band-Aids in assorted sizes
a roll of one-inch gauze and one of two-inch gauze
a roll of one-inch adhesive tape
a box of large sterile gauze pads
an elastic bandage with clips
antiseptic soap
an antiseptic such as hydrogen peroxide
tweezers for slivers
small scissors to cut tape and gauze

If you are In Charge of younger children, you might also need syrup of ipecac and epsom salts. These are used to treat poisoning. A parent can help you decide whether to include these items.

Pack your first aid equipment in a sturdy box—a shoebox or an old lunchbox works well—and label it clearly. Put it on a shelf out of the reach of younger children, and read through the rest of this section. *Relax.* Knowing what to do in an emergency doesn't mean you'll cause one!

Bites

- *If you are bitten by an animal while away from home.* Try to find the animal's owner. Get the owner's complete name, address, and telephone number *and* the name of the

animal's veterinarian. If you can't find the animal's owner, get a full description of the animal and the exact address of the closest house. When you get home, phone the animal-control authority in your city, say that you were bitten, and give a description of the animal and the address.

- *Wash any bite.* Whether animal or human, wash any bite with soap and water.
- *If the bite is bleeding.* Apply direct pressure with a clean cloth or piece of gauze until the bleeding stops (see Bleeding section below).
- *Consult a parent, doctor, or contact neighbor.* Do this immediately for any type of bite. You may need a tetanus shot to prevent infection.

Bleeding

There is bleeding, and there is BLEEDING. Neither one should panic you. It might comfort you to know that, depending on your age and size, you can lose almost a pint of blood without being in serious danger. Here's how to handle each type of bleeding, as well as nosebleeds.

- *Minor bleeding.* From everyday cuts, scratches, and scrapes.

    Press a clean cloth firmly against the wound for three to five minutes until the bleeding stops.

    Wash your hands well.

    Bleeding cleanses the wound so you don't need to wash it. In fact, first aid officials warn that washing it can loosen the clot and cause the wound to bleed again.

Bandage the wound.

If the wound still hurts, wrap an ice cube in a washcloth and hold cloth on top of bandage.

A scrape that does not bleed requires special treatment. Wash it well with antibacterial soap and water. If you've scraped yourself on a gravelly surface, you may need a tetnus shot. Ask an adult.

- *Severe bleeding.* Blood is gushing or spurting and can't be quickly controlled.

Phone for an ambulance. In some cities, it is quicker to phone the police—find out which is preferable in your community.

Control bleeding until help arrives by applying *firm* pressure to the wound with a thick piece of clean cloth.

If possible, raise wound above heart.

Keep victim calm and still—and remain calm yourself—until help arrives.

- *Nosebleeds.* Nosebleeds usually look a lot worse than they are. As with any bleeding, though, it's important to stay calm and get the bleeding stopped.

Keep victim quiet and in a sitting position—with head upright.

Pinch nose—pressing the outside of nostrils toward the center—for ten minutes. Don't let up on the pressure to "check" the bleeding—pinch for a *full* ten minutes.

If this doesn't stop the bleeding, phone a parent or your contact neighbor.

Bumps and Bruises

Unless you spend your life in bed, you're going to get bumped and bruised and banged around. That's just the way it is. Treat everyday bumps and bruises with ice. You can buy an ice compress at the drugstore and keep it in your freezer, or you can make do with ice cubes wrapped in washcloths and plastic bags. In a pinch, you can even get by with bags of frozen food—peas and corn work fine!

If the pain from a bump or bruise doesn't stop after icing it, or if it gets worse or begins to swell, phone for help. Your contact neighbor can help you evaluate the injury if you have doubts.

Pay special attention to bumps on the head. Confusion, severe headache, vomiting, or any loss of consciousness should alert you to call for help immediately!

Burns

Like bleeding, burns come in several types—from minor to serious. Learn to recognize the type, or degree, of burn so that you can treat it properly.

- *First-degree burn—red or discolored skin.*

    Soak burned area in cold water, *not ice*, until the pain stops.

    If the burn is in an area that can't be soaked, apply clean cloths that have been wrung in ice water to it.
- *Second-degree burn—blisters and red, mottled skin.*

    Treat the same as a first-degree burn *unless* it is on a large area, on the face, on hands, or on a joint (elbow, knee, etc.). If this is the case, get emergency help.
- *Third-degree burn—white or charred skin.*

    Phone for an ambulance.

    Don't try to pull off any clothing that is stuck to the burn.

    Don't use water, absorbent cotton, or *any* burn remedies or ointments.

    Do cover the burned area lightly with a clean, dry cloth.

    Use blankets, pillows, coats, or clothing to raise burned arms or legs above heart.

Choking

If you are with someone who begins choking—who cannot speak or breathe or begins to turn blue—use the Heimlich Maneuver. The maneuver, named after its originator, Dr. Henry J. Heimlich, is simple to do and has saved many lives—including the life of the mayor of New York City! Here's how to do it:

- *If the victim is standing.*

    Stand *behind* victim and wrap your arms around victim's waist—just as if you were giving a hug (the Heimlich Maneuver is often called the Heimlich hug).

Make a fist. Don't tuck the thumb in or wrap it around the fist but extend it straight toward the knuckles.

Place the thumb side of your fist toward the victim's abdomen—below the rib cage and just above the navel.

Grab the fist with your other hand.

Push into the victim's abdomen with quick, upward thrusts.

Repeat if necessary.

• *If the victim is sitting.*

Kneel behind victim and use the same method as above.

• *If the victim is lying or has fallen down.*

Kneel astride (across) victim's hips, *facing victim's face.*

Put one hand on top of the other with the heel of the bottom hand on the victim's abdomen—below the rib cage and above the navel.

Using the heel of your hand, press into the victim's abdomen with quick, upward thrusts.

Repeat if necessary.

• *If YOU are choking.*

Press your fist into your abdomen, grasp it with your other hand, and press upward—just as you would with someone else.

You can also lean your abdomen against a chair or table and bring your body quickly and sharply *downward* so that the chair or table pushes quickly and sharply *upward* into your abdomen as the fist ordinarily does in the maneuver.

Choking
The Heimlich Maneuver

Hand position for 1, 2, and 4

1

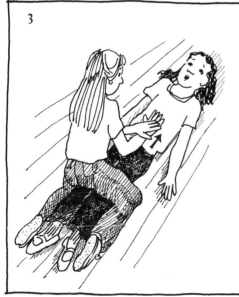

2

3

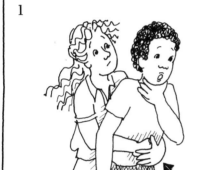

4

Electrical Injury (Electric Shock)

Speed is critical in electrical injury. You must get the victim away from the electric source as quickly as possible, but you must also avoid being shocked yourself. Do not touch the shock victim directly. Here's what to do:

- *Unplug the shock-causing equipment.* If that's not possible, switch off the circuit breaker or remove the fuse that serves that line (for information on circuit breakers and fuses, see the Blackout section, page 36).
- *If you are unable to shut off the equipment.* Stand on a *dry* surface—a blanket, coat, rug, or stack of newspapers will do if the floor is wet—and push the victim away from the power source with a dry board or pole (a broomstick, for example). *Don't* use a pole with metal on it, and *do* make sure your hands are dry.
- *Use a dry rope or cloth.* You can also loop a piece of dry rope or cloth around the victim's hand or arm and pull them away from the power source.
- *Phone for an ambulance.* Do this if the shock victim requires medical help. Get adult advice even if the victim seems fine.

Poisoning

The most important thing you can know about poison treatment is the telephone number of the Poison Control Center closest to your home. Keep the number on or near your telephone.

Follow these steps in the event of poisoning:

1. Give the victim 1–2 glasses of milk or water to dilute the poison. Give milk or water only if the victim is conscious and not vomiting, and don't give *anything* other than milk or water until you have talked to the Poison Control Center.

2. Phone the Poison Control Center. They will tell you what to do until help arrives and will advise you about summoning an ambulance. It will help *them* if you can tell them what poison was taken.

3. Try to find the poison container and take it with the victim to the hospital. If you are unable to find the container and if the victim begins vomiting, save the vomited material in a bag, bowl, or whatever is quickly available and take *it* to the hospital. That sounds really gross, but it can save a life, as the material can be analyzed, the poison pinpointed, and the correct treatment administered.

The labels on containers of poisonous material often suggest antidotes. *Don't* use any of these antidotes without approval from the Poison Control Center, as some of this information is outdated and incorrect, and some of the "cures" are downright dangerous!

Not all poisons are swallowed. Poisonous chemicals can also get on the skin, into eyes, and can be inhaled into the lungs. Here's how to treat these emergencies—

• *Poison on skin:*

Remove clothing from around affected area and rinse with lots of water.

Call Poison Control Center for further treatment.

• *Poison in eyes:*

Don't rub affected eye (or eyes).

Flood eye with warm water, tipping head so that rinse water doesn't wash into other eye.

If both eyes are affected, rinse both with lots of warm water.

Phone for ambulance.

• *Inhaled poisons:*

Get victim to fresh air.

Phone for ambulance.

Illness

An illness isn't usually as dramatic as an injury, but it still deserves your attention.

If you or a child in your care has a headache, sore throat, upset stomach, or other symptom of illness, you'll have to "play doctor" and decide how serious it is and whether an

Who *says* you have to be a gourmet cook to turn out a decent meal? For that matter, who says you have to turn out a *meal* at all? Even the biggest dinner is usually only a meat or a protein thing; a starch thing, like rice, pasta, bread, or potatoes; and a couple of vegetable things. A taco can be all of that in one neat, easy-to-eat package—a hamburger, too.

Meals can be anything as long as they meet nutritional needs. You don't have to prepare a big, fancy meal (unless you want to) if a small, simple meal will do as well. Look at the guidelines below, bear them in mind as you plan your meals, and loosen up! Cooking can be fun.

DAILY NUTRITIONAL NEEDS

Bread/Cereal Group	*Milk Group*	*Protein Group*	
4 or more servings	3–4 cups	Cheese, Meat, Fish, Fowl, Eggs, Nuts, and Beans: 2 or more servings	

Vegetable/Fruit Group
4 or more servings. Include one citrus fruit *daily*
and three dark green vegetables *weekly*

Basics

The rectangular object is the stove—unless, of course, it is the refrigerator. There is usually a difference in temperature that will tell you which is which. After that, things get simpler.

Get to know your kitchen appliances. Ask for lessons in operating the stove, the mixer, the blender, and any other appliances you will use.

Snoop through the cupboards and ask questions. What *is* that funny-looking knife used for? Where are the measuring cups and spoons? Where's the soy sauce, the tomato paste, the peanut butter? Does your household have extra storage for kitchen items in the basement or in a pantry? What's stored *there*? If you know your kitchen well and are comfortable in it, cooking will be easier and a lot more fun.

Planning, Preparation, Cleanup

• *Plan the whole meal before you start any part of it.* If you're going to have spaghetti and salad, take a minute to figure out how long the sauce will simmer, how many min-

utes the pasta should cook, and how long it will take you to make a salad. You might want to write down your time estimates together with a "starting time" for each item.

- *Read recipes and assemble ingredients before beginning.* Check your equipment too. Be sure that you have everything that the recipe calls for.

- *Which ingredients go first?* Some super-efficient cooks line up the ingredients in the order they are called for in the recipe. They then shove them to one side as each is used and don't have to wonder later if they remembered to put the salt in.

- *Always use a cutting board for chopping.*

- *If the food you are cooking needs to be drained.* If oil must be drained off, or if oil or grease remains in the pan after you're done cooking, pour it into an empty can and allow it to cool. *Don't* pour grease down the drain or it will clog the pipes.

- *Watch those hot pots!* Don't set hot pots and pans on countertops or tables without putting down towels or hot-pads first.

- *Clean up as you go.* Wipe counters while the soup heats, rinse dishes while the casserole cooks. It will save you a big, depressing job later.

- *Even if kitchen cleanup isn't your job.* Take a minute to tidy up after yourself. Rinse dirty dishes and stack them neatly, put away ingredients, wipe stove.

Safety

- *Have a fire extinguisher in the kitchen.* And know how to use it.

- *If grease should catch fire in a pan.* Extinguish it with your fire extinguisher, put a heavy lid on the pan to smother the flames, or pour baking soda on it. If you can't put it out right away or if it begins to spread, leave the house and phone the fire department from a neighbor's home.

- *Remember, never use water on a grease or electrical fire.*

- *Get (and use) a kitchen timer.* It will "remind" you when your food is cooked and will keep you from letting pots and pans cook dry.

- *Have oven mitts or potholders by the stove.* And use them.

- *Turn the handles of pots and pans toward the back of the stove.* This will ensure that no one bumps into them and tips them over. Don't put the handles over another hot burner, though, as they can get extremely hot. Plastic handles can even melt and burn.

- *Steam will escape from a covered pot when you lift the lid.* Lift the lid away from you and allow the steam to escape *before* you check on the food. Steam can cause serious burns.

- *If the oven on a gas stove doesn't light.* If the stove doesn't light when you turn it on, turn it off immediately and get help in relighting the pilot.

- *Make sure that your hands are dry when using electrical appliances.* And never use appliances on a wet surface.

- *If you are In Charge of younger children.* Supervise them closely in the kitchen.

Recipes

Here are a few recipes to start you thinking. Use them, adjust them to your taste, invent your own creations, and start collecting other recipes for quick and easy dishes. Ask other In Charge kids for *their* recipes and start your own recipe file.

Incidentally, most of the breakfast suggestions taste just as good at noon or 6 P.M. as they do in the morning, and many of the lunch suggestions would make a fine breakfast, or two or three together would make a tasty dinner.

Breakfast

Fried eggs aren't the final word. A lot of people live long and healthy lives without eating eggs or bacon or toast for breakfast. Some people eat cheese, bread, and fruit in the morning; some eat yogurt; some eat tacos. It's important to eat something nutritious every morning, but it doesn't have to be steak and eggs. Be creative!

Simple Stuff

- Slice any kind of fruit into a bowl. Top with yogurt and coconut—or raisins or nuts or granola or all of them. Next time, try berries or pitted cherries. Add cinnamon. Add honey. Add vanilla. Soon you'll be mixing it up in the bathtub and feeding the whole neighborhood.
- Peel an orange. Chop it up and mix it with cottage cheese. Use a chopped pear instead, or canned, drained pineapple. Try all three together for an exotic fruit salad.
- Make a peanut butter, banana, and honey sandwich on whole wheat, or on raisin bread or toast.
- Slice an apple. Eat it with cheese chunks and bread, or dip apple slices into cinnamon-spiced yogurt and eat them with a piece of toast.
- Toast a bagel, then top it with cream cheese and apple or banana slices.
- Split pita (pocket) bread. Fill with cream cheese and berries, cheese and apples, or cream cheese and walnuts. Put your whole breakfast into the pita pocket and eat it on the run if you're late.

Blender Breakfasts

Blend these on "high" for a minute or so. Each recipe makes one serving.

BERRY-CHERRY-FRUIT SHAKE

1 *cup chopped fruit, berries, or pitted cherries (try one*
   kind or a mixture)
1 *cup yogurt*
1 *tablespoon honey (optional)*

Put everything into the blender jar. Cover and blend.

BANANA-GRAPE SHAKE

1 peeled banana
2 tablespoons frozen grape juice concentrate
1 cup yogurt

Break peeled banana into pieces. Put it, the yogurt, and the grape concentrate into blender jar. Cover and blend.

PEANUT BUTTER-BANANA SHAKE

1 peeled banana
3 tablespoons peanut butter
1 cup yogurt
1 tablespoon honey (optional)

Put everything into blender jar. Cover and blend.

FRUIT-MILK SHAKE

1 cup fruit juice, any kind
½ cup milk
¼ cup dry milk powder

Put everything into blender jar. Cover and blend.

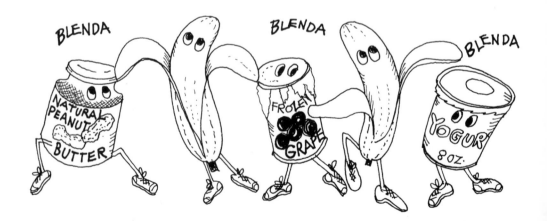

Sunday Specials

These are for days when you have a little extra time.

SCRAMBLED EGGS PLUS *(serves 1)*

2 eggs
1 teaspoon milk
1 tablespoon butter or margarine

Break eggs into small bowl. Add milk. Mix well with beater or fork.

Melt butter or margarine in small skillet over low heat. Add eggs to pan, stir, and cook until eggs are thick but still moist. Remove pan from heat.

VARIATION: Have some fun with your eggs. Top them with chopped tomatoes, grated cheese, chopped mushrooms, chopped green pepper, or whatever sounds good to you.

Double or triple this recipe to make breakfast for the whole family.

FRENCH TOAST *(serves 4)*

4 eggs
½ cup milk (or cream for a special treat)
¼ teaspoon salt (optional)
½ teaspoon vanilla extract or a sprinkling of cinnamon
 (both optional)
2 tablespoons butter or margarine
10 slices bread ("day-old" bread works best)

Break eggs into bowl. Beat with a hand beater until bubbly. Add milk, salt, and vanilla. Beat again.

Melt a little of the butter or margarine in a griddle, in an electric frypan, or in a skillet over medium heat. Divide the 2 tablespoons of butter between the number of batches you will have to cook to use all the bread.

Dip the bread quickly into the egg batter and fry on both sides until golden brown.

Butter the pan after each batch of toast.

Serve with syrup, jam or jelly, honey, or sprinkle toast with powdered sugar and put lemon wedges on the table to squeeze over toast.

Lunches

Lunch doesn't have to be a peanut butter and jelly sandwich in a crumpled bag. Make your lunches as exciting as your breakfasts.

• *Yogurt and fruit.* Put one of your yogurt and fruit (or cottage cheese and fruit) creations in a plastic or thermal container for lunch.

- *Slice some cheese; pack crackers and sliced raw vegetables.*
- *Make your own cheese spread.* Use it on bread or crackers or to stuff celery with. To make the spread: Put one package (8 ounces) cream cheese into a small bowl. Add one cup grated Cheddar (or another favorite) cheese. Allow cheeses to stand at room temperature until softened. Add ½ tablespoon Worcestershire sauce. Blend ingredients together with a wooden spoon (or mash together with a potato masher).

   You can add other things to this mix to spice it up. If you leave out the Worcestershire sauce, you can put in chopped walnuts, raisins, and drained crushed pineapple. Or leave in the Worcestershire and add chopped onions and olives or sunflower seeds. This mix keeps well in the refrigerator and you can use it for several lunches, breakfasts, or snacks. If you take out the amount you need in advance and let it sit at room temperature, it will soften and be easier to spread.

- *Experiment with bread.* Pita (pocket) bread is wonderful. You can fill it with anything for an easy lunch. Try a tuna spread—tuna mixed with pickle relish or celery and salad dressing or mayonnaise—or fill the pita with your own cheese spread. Stuff it with cream cheese and jam or with avocado mashed with a little lemon juice (and salt, if you want) and mixed with sprouts or olives. Try a tuna sandwich on a hamburger bun or an onion roll and a peanut butter sandwich on raisin bread. Look around the bread section of your supermarket. What looks good?

- *Plan ahead.* One way to make sure that you don't slip into the same sandwich-in-a-crumpled-bag routine is to plan ahead and do as much as possible in advance.

Keep your lunch-making supplies—sandwich bags, lunch bags, plastic containers, etc.—together on a shelf or in a drawer in the kitchen.

Always keep fruit in the refrigerator or cupboard.

If you take a dessert other than fruit in your lunch, try wrapping or bagging a week's supply of cookies in advance. Stack the wrapped cookies with your lunch-making supplies. It's reassuring to know that you have cookies and an apple or a banana stashed away. All you need to do is make a sandwich and you're ready to go.

If you're really organized, you can make a lot of sandwiches on a rainy Saturday and freeze them. The nice

thing about frozen sandwiches is that they don't have to be thawed before you pack them. Put them into your lunch bag frozen, and they'll thaw out by lunchtime. As a bonus, they'll be nice and cold. Cheese, peanut butter and sliced meats all freeze well. Mayonnaise, salad dressing, jam or jelly, eggs, and fresh vegetables *don't*. If you want to freeze tuna sandwiches, moisten the tuna with pickle relish and/or sour cream rather than with mayonnaise or salad dressing. *Don't* freeze lettuce in sandwiches. Put the lettuce in when you take the sandwich from the freezer, or put the lettuce in a plastic bag and add it at lunchtime.

You can also make your sandwich before going to bed, put it into a sandwich bag, and refrigerate it overnight. If you decide to do this, and are using a moist filling, spread the inside of the bread with a *thin* layer of softened butter to "seal" the filling in and keep the bread from getting soggy.

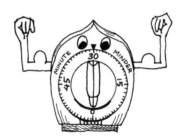

Dinners

These dinners are "30-minute wonder meals." None takes much over a half hour to cook, they all taste great, and served with suggested accompaniments, they all meet basic nutritional needs.

An easy way to balance your dinners nutritionally is to "cook by color." Include something green and something either yellow, orange, or red with your main dish.

TACO SALAD *(serves 4–6, depending upon appetites)*

This Taco Salad is a balanced meal by itself. You can serve something with it, but you don't have to.

1 can (15 ounces) kidney beans
1 medium-size head lettuce (any kind)
1 or 2 tomatoes
1 or 2 green peppers
1 cucumber
4 or 5 green onions
1½ cups grated Cheddar or Monterey Jack cheese
1 cup crushed tortilla chips
1 pound ground beef
¼ to ½ cup of bottled French-style salad dressing, or
  make your own salad dressing (see page 84)

Put kidney beans in strainer and rinse well under cold water. Wash lettuce, pat dry with paper towels, chop or tear into large bowl. Wash, and peel if necessary, other vegetables. Add to lettuce in bowl. Add cheese, beans, and crushed tortilla chips to bowl (save a few to decorate salad).

Brown ground beef. Put it in pan over medium heat, break up with spoon, and cook, stirring constantly, until meat loses its pink color but *not* until it gets crispy.

Remove pan from heat. Remove meat from pan with slotted spoon so that grease drains off. Add meat to salad.

Add ¼ to ½ cup of salad dressing (or enough to suit your family's taste) and toss. Decorate the top of salad with tortilla chips and serve.

POCKET TACOS   (serves 4)

Here is another taco-style recipe. Serve it with a plate of carrot or celery sticks, and you'll have a complete meal.

3 or 4 cups chopped lettuce
1 or 2 chopped tomatoes
1 small chopped onion
2 or 3 cups grated Cheddar or Monterey Jack cheese
1 package pita bread
1 pound ground beef
1 envelope taco seasoning
1 cup sour cream
Bottled taco sauce or salsa

Arrange the lettuce, tomatoes, onion, and cheese on a platter. Cut the pita bread in half and put it in a basket or bowl or on a plate.

Brown the ground beef: Put it in pan over medium heat, break up with spoon, and cook, stirring constantly, until meat loses its pink color but *not* until it's crispy. Add seasoning. Stir well to mix.

Remove the pan from heat. Remove the meat from the pan, using a slotted spoon so that the grease can run off.

Put the meat in a bowl and let everyone make their own pocket tacos. Pass the sour cream and taco sauce.

VARIATION: You can make your own taco seasoning with a dash of pepper, a teaspoon of cumin, a teaspoon of oregano, a pinch of garlic powder (or a chopped garlic clove), and a dash of salt. Experiment with other ingredients until you find a seasoning tailor-made for your tastes.

SUPER SPUDS (serves 4)

A baked potato is like the foundation for a house—once it's down, you can build on it. Here are some ideas to get you going. Serve Super Spuds with a salad and a green vegetable.

4 large baking potatoes
1 can chili (size of can depends upon appetites)
3 cups grated Cheddar or Monterey Jack cheese
1 small chopped yellow onion or 4 chopped green onions
1 cup sour cream

Preheat oven to 350 degrees.

Scrub the potatoes well. Pat dry with paper towels. Prick potatoes 2 or 3 times with the tines of a fork so that steam can escape while they are cooking.

Bake the potatoes 1½ to 2 hours at 350 degrees. Smaller potatoes will cook faster. Baked potatoes are done when you can squish them (be sure to wear an oven mitt).

When the potatoes are almost done, heat the chili in a pan, then pour it into a bowl.

Put bowls of cheese, chopped onion, and sour cream on the table and let everyone build their own Super Spud.

SURPRISE BURGERS   *(serves 4)*

Everyone loves a burger. This one has a surprise inside. Serve with carrots, celery, pickles, and olives.

1 pound ground beef
4 slices Cheddar, or Monterey Jack, or Swiss cheese
4 thin slices yellow onion
4 lettuce leaves
4 hamburger buns or onion rolls

Divide meat into eight patties (four for the bottom, four for the top). Top each patty "bottom" with a slice of cheese and a slice of onion. Put on "top" patty and flatten the meat to completely cover the cheese and onion. Pinch edges to seal the "surprise" inside.

Cook meat under oven broiler 7 minutes on each side, *or* fry in pan over medium heat 10 minutes on each side.

Serve on lettuce-lined rolls *or* buns. You can toast the rolls if you prefer.

VARIATION: Leave out the onion if you don't like onions. Add things you do like. What else can be sealed up in your Surprise Burgers? How about mushrooms and olives?

TUNA CHOW MEIN   (*serves 4*)

Tuna Chow Mein is a simple dinner that is complete if served with a salad.

2 stalks celery
½ small onion
1 small green pepper
½ can (5½ ounces) chow mein noodles
1 can (6½ ounces) tuna
1 can (10½ ounces) cream of mushroom soup
½ cup milk
2 tablespoons soy sauce
Salt and pepper (optional)

Preheat oven to 350 degrees. Lightly butter a 1½-quart casserole.

Chop celery, onion, and green pepper. Reserving ¼ cup noodles, put all other ingredients into casserole. Mix. Sprinkle the reserved ¼ cup noodles on top of casserole.

Bake casserole, uncovered, for 30 minutes.

VARIATION: You can add other ingredients to this casserole. Try putting in a small package of thawed frozen peas, *or* some sliced mushrooms, *or* some almonds (*or* add all three).

NOTE: If you don't want to use canned soup as a sauce, you can make your own sauce by melting 2 tablespoons butter in a pan over low heat. When butter has melted, add 1½ to 2 tablespoons flour. Stir, over low heat, for 3 minutes (or until ingredients are well mixed). Slowly pour in 1 cup of milk and continue to stir (with a wire whisk, if your kitchen has one) until the mixture simmers, thickens, and is smooth. Add to casserole instead of the soup. (You can add chopped mushrooms and/or chopped parsley to flavor your sauce, if you wish.)

Salads

Lettuce begin! A salad is a wonderful thing limited only by your imagination (which is probably not very limited at all). Lettuce is *only* the beginning, and even lettuce is not just *lettuce*. Try red leaf, romaine, endive, fresh spinach, or butter lettuce. Shop around your supermarket and try something new.

Salads can be a main course or a side dish. They don't require a stove or careful measuring. Here are a few simple salad recommendations.

- Wash all vegetables well in cold water; pat dry with paper towels.

- Add cheese, tuna, olives, leftover meat, and mushrooms to salads. Put in things you like, leave out things you don't.
- Pour on salad dressing just before serving.
- Make your own salad dressing (see below).

SALAD DRESSING

3 tablespoons olive or vegetable oil
1 tablespoon lemon juice or vinegar
Salt
¼ teaspoon dry mustard (optional)

Combine all ingredients in a small jar. Cover and shake well.

This recipe makes enough dressing for a small salad for three or four people, but you can double the recipe or quadruple it. In fact, all you really need to remember to make a good salad dressing is to use three parts oil (3 tablespoons or cups or whatever) to one part (1 tablespoon or cup or whatever) lemon juice or vinegar. Even this varies, for some people always use *four* parts oil to one part lemon juice or vinegar. Use the proportions that taste best to *you* and add your favorite herbs, condiments, and "extras" to make the salad dressing suit you.

VARIATION: Try a pinch of poppy *or* celery seeds, a clove of crushed garlic, a pinch of curry powder *or* paprika, some grated onion, crumbled Roquefort cheese, *or* some Worcestershire sauce.

You can also dress a salad with a simple splash of lemon juice and a dash of salt and pepper. Less is sometimes better, especially if your vegetables are fresh and cold.

You don't have to serve lettuce to have a good salad. Here are a few other suggestions:

- Grate a few scrubbed carrots, add raisins, and toss with yogurt or sour cream.
- Wash some apples. Chop the apples, some walnuts, and a few stalks of celery. Dress with salad dressing, yogurt and honey, or sour cream.
- Fill a fresh or canned pear half with cottage cheese, yogurt, or grated cheese (any kind).

Snacks

Fix simple, healthy snacks for after school or between meals.

- Make one of your yogurt and fruit creations or a blender-built yogurt shake.
- Eat some fruit. Dip it in yogurt or eat it with cheese slices.
- Stuff celery stalks with peanut butter or with some of your own cheese spread.
- Put some of the cheese spread on bread and melt it under the broiler for a minute or two.
- Or try one of the following:

CAROB SHAKE-IN-A-JAR (serves 1)

1 cup milk
1 tablespoon instant dry milk powder
1½ tablespoons carob powder
1 tablespoon honey
¼ teaspoon vanilla
1 shake cinnamon

Put all ingredients in a jar. Cover jar and shake until everything is mixed.

POPCORN

¼ cup popcorn kernels
2 tablespoons vegetable oil

Put oil into large saucepan that has a tight-fitting lid. Put three "trial" kernels of corn into pan, cover, and put on burner. Heat, on medium, until trial kernels pop.

Remove pan from heat, lift lid carefully, and add ¼ cup kernels. Cover pan, shake quickly, and return pan to burner. When corn begins to pop, shake back and forth rapidly over the burner until the popping stops.

Remove pan from heat. Lift lid *carefully.*

VARIATION: You can add Parmesan cheese, grated Cheddar, or seasoned salt to make your popcorn more exciting. But if you're a popcorn purist, just add salt and eat.

MINI-PIZZA   *(serves 1)*

1 English muffin, split in half
1 or 2 tablespoons canned or bottled tomato sauce
Oregano
Mozzarella cheese (or American or Swiss cheese)
Parmesan cheese

Preheat oven to 400 degrees.

Brush muffin tops with tomato sauce. Sprinkle with oregano. Cover with slices of cheese. Sprinkle with Parmesan cheese.

Put muffins on cookie sheet or in a shallow baking pan and put in oven for 5 minutes (or until hot).

VARIATIONS: Add chopped olives, pepperoni, green pepper,

or onions. You can make several mini-pizzas and serve with a
big salad for dinner.

APPLE TOAST

Preheat oven to 375 degrees.

Butter 2 slices of bread or 2 split English muffins.

Wash, dry, and thinly slice 1 small apple. Put ¼ of the
apple slices on each piece of bread or muffin half. (Eat the rest
of the apple.) Sprinkle cinnamon on top. Bake 10 to 12 minutes.

Apple toast is especially good on a cold day with cocoa or
hot spiced cider, but it's not bad on a hot day with a glass of
cold water either.

Would you like to learn more about cooking? Many schools
and clubs offer cooking classes, and there are wonderful cook-
books for chefs of all ages. Check your library.

4. CARING FOR YOUR CLOTHES

Laundering

Ironing

Mending

Okay, now you've eaten. The next step is to get dressed. If you're going to be In Charge, a good place to start is with your own clothes. They're yours, after all. No one else wrinkles them, rips them, grows into and out of them. And clothes are actually pretty easy to take care of—they just hang around, and they *never* talk back.

Laundering

If you are going to take charge of your own laundry, you'll need to learn how to operate the washer and dryer. Every machine works a little differently, and this book can give you only general instructions. Ask an adult in your household for specifics—how to operate the machines, where the laundry soap is stored, what can be washed (and with what), and what should *never* be washed under any circumstances. Take notes so that you can consult them later if you have doubts.

General Directions

- *Separate your clothes.* Separate them according to color and fabric type. For example, put dark clothes on one pile, whites on another; put jeans on one stack, delicate fabrics on another.

- *Always wash new dark or bright clothes separately.* Bright and dark colors often fade—leak dye—during the first few washings. You only have to wear pink underwear to gym once to understand the importance of washing a red sweatshirt by itself the first few times.

- *Empty all pockets* (shirt pockets too). Experiments, accidentally conducted in many homes, have shown that felt-tip pens and crayons make a particularly awful mess when washed and dried.

- *Check the label.* If you aren't sure if a garment can be washed, check the label. There are usually "care instructions" at the neckline of shirts (check the reverse side of the size label) and inside the waistband of pants. Occasionally, manufacturers put care labels inside the side seam. If, after careful searching, you can't find the care instructions and you're not sure about washability, put the garment aside and wait for expert advice. The safest rule for laundry is: When in doubt, leave it out!

- *Stains.* Treat stains with prewashing liquid or spray. If you don't have a prewash, rub a little liquid detergent or even shampoo into the stain before washing. Incidentally, it is easier to remove stains if you deal with them promptly. *Don't* allow them to take up permanent residence in your clothes.

- *Decide whether to use cold or hot water.* Read the deter-

gent box or your garment's care labels or ask an adult if you have doubts about what temperature clothes should be washed in.

- *Follow detergent instructions to the letter.* This isn't a good time to be creative. Add *exactly* as much detergent as the instructions call for and at *exactly* the point in the wash cycle that it is called for.

- *Be particularly careful if you use bleach. Never* pour liquid bleach directly onto clothes or add clothes to undiluted bleach, or it will eat amazing holes in them. Bleach bottles contain directions for dilution. Follow them carefully. It is helpful to keep an old measuring cup by the washing machine to measure bleach or detergent.

- *Once the wash load is going.* Don't open the lid without turning the washer off. Some machines automatically stop spinning when the lid is raised, but don't take any chances.
- *After the clothes are washed.* Hang them on a clothesline or dry them in the dryer. Again, get lessons if you're going to use the dryer.
- *Clean the dryer's lint trap after each use to avoid fire.*
- *Some clothes can be machine-washed but not machine-dried.* If you aren't sure if your clothes can be machine-dried, play it safe and hang them on the clothesline or over the shower rod to dry.
- *If you use the dryer.* Remove clothes as soon as they're dry. Hang or fold clothes immediately to avoid wrinkling.

Ironing

You shouldn't have much ironing if you remove your clothes from the dryer promptly and smooth them with your hands. If you do need to iron, get lessons first, and remember these tips:

- Use the correct temperature setting for the garment you are ironing. Many irons have settings for "wool," "cotton," and "permanent press," and most clothes have labels listing their fiber content so that all you have to do is match them up. If your iron doesn't have a temperature setting guide or if you can't find your garment's fiber content, ask for adult help.
- Fill the iron's "water well" if you are going to use steam or spray. *Unplug the iron* when filling or refilling the well.

- Iron with a light touch. The heat will remove the wrinkles—you don't need to rely upon brute force.
- *Don't* use the iron if the cord is frayed or the plug loose.
- Unplug the iron when you are finished using it and let it cool on a heat-resistant surface—a stove or similar surface—before you put it away.
- If you are In Charge of younger children (or pets), don't leave the iron plugged in if you leave the room. Take time to unplug it and put it (with its cord) well out of reach, even if you're only going to be gone a minute.

Mending

A stitch in time can save your social standing. Especially if it's the stitch that holds your pants up or your shirt on.

Before you can start sewing, you need to gather a few tools.

Sewing Kit

If your household has a family sewing kit, you won't need a kit of your own, but if no other kit is available, put one together yourself. Include:

Needles: a package of "sharps" in assorted sizes.

Straight pins: you'll need a couple of dozen to hold hems and seams in place while you are sewing.

Safety pins: a dozen or so in assorted sizes, good for emergency repairs.

A small pincushion to keep pins and needles together.

A few spools of thread: black, white, navy blue, and whatever other color(s) you wear a lot.

A pair of sewing scissors: unless you're planning to get into sewing in a big way, you can get by with a small pair—but they should be sharp.

A couple of pieces of chalk to mark hems: you can buy dressmaker or tailor's chalk or you can get by with blackboard chalk.

A ruler or tape measure.

A big package of iron-on patches in assorted colors.

Basic Sewing Skills

There are a few things you need to know before you can take charge of your mending. Ask someone—an adult or another kid—to teach you how to thread a needle, knot the thread, and tie off the thread if you don't already know how to do these things. Practice these skills and then ask to be taught two or three simple stitches. It will be useful for you to know how to do a "running" stitch and a "backstitch," as well as a "hemming" stitch. None of these stitches is hard to learn—just be sure that you understand the instructions (see page 98). It might help if your "teacher" does a few sample stitches on a scrap of cloth that you can keep and look at later if you get confused.

What if you can't find anyone to teach you to sew? Have you *really* looked? Try your school's home economics teacher (or a student in the home ec. class) or a neighbor or a relative. If you still can't locate a willing teacher, check your library. There are several good books available to help kids learn to sew. Read one of these books, follow the diagrams, and practice, practice, practice.

Remember to keep your stitches small and fairly close together and firm but *not* so tight that they pucker the fabric.

When you're satisfied with your practice stitches, you're ready to use your new skills to keep your wardrobe looking good.

Repairs

The Ups and Downs of Hemming

• Mark the hem. Try on the pants, skirt, or dress and have

Basic Stitches

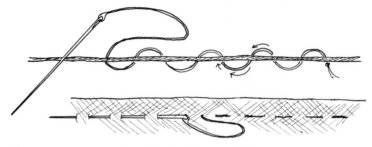

RUNNING STITCH
A fast, simple stitch—good for basting

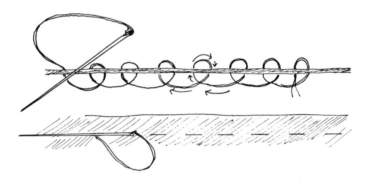

BACKSTITCH
A strong stitch—good for seams and areas that get lots of wear

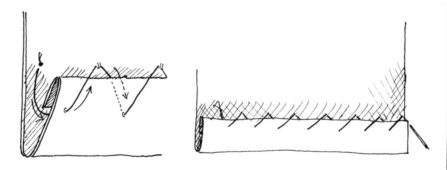

HEMMING STITCH
For hems—this stitch is nearly invisible on the outside of garment

someone mark the new hem for you with chalk or pins. If no one is available to help, you can lay the garment on a table and smooth it out. Now lay a pair of pants, dress, or skirt that *are* the right length on top of the new garment. Mark the new garment with chalk or pins.

- If a garment needs a huge hem, you will probably have to get adult help. Huge hems look strange, and you will do better to cut away some of the excess fabric before you hem.
- Turn the hem to the inside, measuring to keep it straight. Pin into place, press it, and watching out for pins, try it on. *Make sure* that you like the new length before you start sewing. Look at it in a full-length mirror if you have one.
- Hem, using a hemming stitch.

Rip in Seam

- If a seam—the place where two pieces of fabric are

joined—comes apart, put it back together again with a running stitch or a backstitch.

- Pin the pieces together so that they don't slip while you are sewing.
- Make small, even stitches.
- Use a thread color closely matched to the color of the garment.

Patches

- When the knee on your jeans gives out or you get a tear that isn't on a seam, it's time to break out the iron-on patches in your sewing kit.

- Match the patch color closely to the garment color.
- Follow the directions on the patch package.
- You can apply patches to the inside of the garment, and they will hardly show at all.
- If you love to sew, or want to do some creative patching, you can sew on a decorative patch you make yourself:

   Use a scrap of fabric similar in weight to the fabric of the garment you are mending. (You can buy small pieces of fabric in the remnant bins of many fabric stores.)

Cut a simple shape out of the scrap fabric (a kite, a heart, a flower or another easy-to-cut shape). Pin the edges under (about ¼ inch) and iron in a temporary "hem."

Pin patch in place on garment and sew around edges, using a running stitch or backstitch. (Try using a contrasting color of thread for added pizzaz.) You can also buy fusible webbing at a fabric store that allows you to join two pieces of fabric together using your iron. Be sure to follow the instructions exactly if you use this product!

Buttons

- Save all buttons. If you find a button in the washer, dryer, on the kitchen floor, or wherever, save it. Someone, someday, will want it. Get a little box and put stray buttons in it.
- When you notice that your favorite shirt is missing a button, go to your button box—aren't you glad that you have one?—and find the missing button or one that is very close

in size and color to the other buttons on your shirt. If you can't find a button that looks like the remaining buttons, you will have to go to a fabric, variety, or department store and buy a replacement button. Try to find a store that sells single buttons—it's expensive and time-consuming to replace *all* the buttons.

• Once you have a replacement, find out exactly where it belongs. Usually a button leaves little holes behind when it falls off. If that's the case, all you need to do is sew the button on over the holes. If the holes have vanished along with the button, button all the other buttons on your garment. The empty buttonhole will direct you to the missing button's proper place.

• Use a double thread and take five to six stitches through the holes in the button so that it is firmly in place. Be sure to keep stitches neat, not lumpy.

Can you think of other ways to take charge of your clothing? Hang clothing up promptly on an appropriate hanger (there are hangers suited to almost every type of garment) or smooth wrinkles out with your hand and fold (for sweaters and knits) to avoid ironing; treat stains to ward off permanent spots; and be careful not to overdry your clothes. If you have clothing that requires dry cleaning, you should learn how to prepare it for cleaning (empty pockets, pretreat spots, etc.), and you should know which dry cleaner your family uses. You should also take responsibility for keeping an "inventory" of your clothing needs or necessary professional repairs. If your jeans are too tight or your shoes are coming apart, *you* need to make a note of it and tell an adult.

5. CHARGING AHEAD

I t's time for a long look back at how far you've come. You've learned how to be a "full partner" in your working family. You know what your family expects of you and what you can expect of them. You know which chores to do and when to do them. You've learned when and where to get help if you need it and how to organize your time and space to suit your busy life. You've read about hemming jeans and giving the Heimlich hug, about hassle-free cooking and tangle-free sewing.

Think about all the things you've accomplished and the situations you feel competent to handle now. List them. This is your personal stockpile of survival skills—one you will be adding to all your life.

Are there areas you're still unsure of? List *them*. Find ways to gain skills to help you overcome your doubts.

Does the sight, or the thought, of blood still make you dizzy? Take some first aid classes.

Are you still frightened by crime reports? If you are, admit it and do something to gain control of the situation. Ask your parents to hold a neighborhood "crimewatch" meeting. Many police departments will help you set one up and will often send a speaker to tell neighbors how to protect themselves and one another. Make sure it isn't an "adults only" affair. All In Charge kids need to be involved in crime prevention!

If you're still apprehensive, take personal defense classes. They're great exercise and a good way to gain confidence and body awareness as well as to learn personal safety skills. Check for classes at your local Parks (or Police) Department, the YWCA, YMHA, or YMCA, or with the Scouts or a similar organization.

Call for regular family conferences. These conferences can be a relaxed chat over dinner or something more formal, but it's important to keep them up. Family schedules and needs change, and you will want to keep your information current.

A family conference is a good time to talk about *your* needs too. Are you feeling okay about your situation, or do you feel that household work is unfairly distributed or that you are not able to do what is expected of you? Do you *understand* what is expected of you? Are you able to do your household chores and still keep up with your schoolwork? If your chore schedule is making it difficult to complete your homework, discuss the problem with your family. Are you comfortable with your role when you are In Charge? Can you keep the peace between brothers, sisters, and yourself? Do you have a workable, fair system for resolving arguments? Are you able to enforce the house rules? Do you know what to do (and can you do it?) if a friend, or the friend of a brother or sister, disregards your family's rules?

Be honest. It may be hard to admit that you are having problems or that your family's system is not working for you. It's especially hard to admit if *you* helped design the system, but it's far *more* difficult to struggle each day with too many

chores or too much responsibility or too little organization. Discuss your uncertainty, frustration, or confusion with your family. Let them help you "grow into" your role. The kind of growing you're doing, from dependence to *in*dependence, will continue throughout your life, and you're sure to need help at many points along the way.

Sometimes asking for help is the most mature and responsible thing you can do, and you should *never* feel that asking for advice or assistance is the same as admitting failure. Slowing down—even changing directions—is not the same thing as stopping!

You need to keep in mind the progress you've made, especially when you're having problems. Think back to a year ago, or a month ago, and remember all the things you "couldn't" do and had to depend upon others to do for you. Think about how many of those things you can do on your own now. It's probably an impressive list of achievements.

Pat yourself on the back. It hasn't always been easy, but you've stuck with it. And *look* at how far you've come—all the way from being alone to being In Charge.

Bibliography

CHILD CARE

Herzig, Alison Cragin, and Mali, Jane Lawrence. *Oh, Boy! Babies!* Boston: Little, Brown 1980.

> This book shows the workings of an unusual course in child care—a course that used real babies and where all the students were fifth- and sixth-grade boys. The book has a lot of practical ideas, wonderful photographs by Katrina Thomas, *and* a fresh look at boys as baby-sitters.

Saunders, Rubie. *The Franklin Watts Concise Guide to Baby-Sitting.* New York: Franklin Watts 1972.

> This is a useful book if you're sitting for a child in your family *or* as a paying job. There are checklists, charts, and suggestions to help you streamline your child-care responsibilities.

COOKING

Stein, Sara Bonnett. *The Kid's Kitchen Takeover.* New York: Workman Publishing 1975.

> Grow herbs in your kitchen or an avocado in your window, make cookies or jelly or jewelry or candles—this book will help you do it all (and more). There are lots of wonderful facts, terrific photographs by Dick Frank, and enough ideas to keep you cooking and creating for weeks.

Gaeddert, Louann. *Your Night to Make Dinner.* New York: Franklin Watts, 1977.

> There are helpful hints on meal planning and shopping in this book, as well as lots of recipes. There's even a "Speedy Special" chapter with recipes for meals you can prepare in less than thirty minutes.

FIRST AID

American Red Cross. *Standard First Aid and Personal Safety.* 2nd ed. Garden City, NY: Doubleday, 1979.

> This is a serious, straightforward book that is a good reference to have in your first aid kit and is helpful reading if you can't take a first aid course but want to sharpen your emergency skills.

Boy Scouts of America. *First Aid.* BSA, 1981.

> This is a useful, inexpensive first aid book that would also make a nice addition to your home first aid kit. The Boy Scouts also publish a book on safety and accident prevention.

FOOD

US Department of Agriculture. *What's to Eat? And Other Questions Kids Ask About Food.* Washington, D.C.: Government Printing Office, 1979.

> This book uses quizzes, riddles, charts, illustrations, and photographs to teach about food, nutrition and smart shopping. There are recipes too.

Bernick, Deborah, and Bershad, Carol. *Bodyworks: The Kid's Guide to Food and Physical Fitness.* New York: Random House, 1979.

> The purpose of this book is to help you get and stay healthy through sensible eating and exercise. There are food tips, ideas for games and exercises, and great illustrations by Heidi Johanna Selig.

SEWING

Barkin, Carol, and James, Eliza. *Slapdash Sewing.* New York: Lothrop, Lee & Shepherd, 1975.

> These authors use the "no-sweat" approach to sewing and can guide you through any of your sewing projects.

Index

Stomachaches, 60–61
Storage
  clothes, 30
  kitchen, 66
Stoves, lighting, 69
Strangers, 46–50
  delivery persons, 47–48
  at the door, 46–48
  on the phone, 48–49
  prowlers, 49–50
Superintendent, apartment
  lockout and, 36
  phone number of, 8
  plumbing problems and, 39
  power outage and, 38
Supplies
  family organization, 21–22
  lunch-making, 76
  school, 30–31
Swellings, 54

t

Taco recipes. *See* Dinner recipes: Pocket
  Tacos
Telephone
  list of important numbers, 7–9
  rules for using, 4–5
  strangers and, 48–49
Television, rules for using, 4–5

Time schedule, 24–28
  sample, 26
Toilet overflow, 39
"Tool kit," In Charge, 19–22

V

Veterinarian, 9
Vomiting, 54, 61
  in poisoning, 59

W

Washer, clothes, 91, 94
Water
  shutoff valves, 38–39
  to use in laundry, 92–93

y

Yogurt recipes, 70–72, 74, 85
Younger children
  authority over, 6
  fire drill for, 41
  Fire escape with, 43
  first aid for, 51
  house rules for, 5
  irons and, 95
  in-kitchen supervision of, 69
  medicines and, 61

Kathy S. Kyte

was born in Reno, Nevada and grew up in Eugene, Oregon. She attended the University of Oregon in Eugene and graduated with a B.S. degree in communications and journalism from Lewis and Clark College in Portland. Her published work includes newspaper feature articles, fiction and poetry.

Ms. Kyte lives with her husband, Michael Kyte, and her two children, Brendan and Brooke Williams, in Iowa City, where she is a graduate student in fiction at the Iowa Writers' Workshop.